What Our Readers Have Said...

"Although I consider myself a seasoned sales professional, it is helpful to have past learning's refreshed. The books were also beneficial because of the information concerning 'trends' in the sales relationship. The sales process should be viewed as dynamic since business relationships change regularly."

•

"For the particular business I am in and the type of sales calls I have, I find that the books in the Pinpoint Sales Training Series are very often applicable to how I conduct business. I would recommend them to other sales people, just not ones that are in my industry."

•

"These books provide very good concepts. It fits in well with the Bell Leadership training program that I attended in November."

•

"I use this material in these books and apply it to my customers and other employees I work with."

•

"I would like to know other topics. Is there anything on Production Management or Consultative Selling or Time Management?"

•

"These books are great tools that should be used as guidelines for our everyday

supervisory practices. You need to take the time to do a short self-evaluation when reading them."

•

"The Pinpoint Training Series delivers information that could be used in a lot different areas."

•

"I like this because I can take them with me to read at a convenient time. I feel the little time I have to spend in the office is best use on activities that directly relate to revenue opportunities. I like the short amount of time it takes to keep up with these."

•

"I prefer the self-study approach; it fits in with my schedule."

•

"My thought is that the real value of these books comes into effect when doing the action plans."

•

"Short and sweet. These books are easy to comprehend."

•

"I have enjoyed reading these books. They are relevant to today's work environment and the ongoing change in the way we manage our workforce."

•

"I do feel that these books have been very helpful to me at my job."

•

"I think a lot of the recommendations in these books are very useful, and can be applicable to everyday situations. If nothing else, it's a good reference guide to fall back upon if a situation arises in the future."

•

"These books are relevant to today's work environment and the ongoing change in the way we manage our workforce."

•

Cultivating Customer Confidence

Pinpoint Sales Skill Development Training Series

TIMOTHY F. BEDNARZ

MAJORIUM
BUSINESS PRESS

Pinpoint Sales Skill Development Training Series
"Cultivating Customer Confidence"
Timothy F. Bednarz

Graphic design: Monika Pawlak

Majorium Business Press
2025 Main Street
Stevens Point, WI 54481
715.342.1018 • 800.654.4935

ISBN 978-1-882181-84-1

Printed in the United States of America

Introduction

The Pinpoint Sales Skill Development Training Series is designed for targeted training and education regarding increased improvement in a specific skill or competency.

Each book within this series is designed to be easy to use, understand and apply to your job. It can be used as a basis for training individuals, as a discussion guide or as a personal training tool.

Each chapter within this book discusses a specific concept. When you have completed all eight chapters you should have a 360° perspective of the topic.

Additionally, each chapter is divided into specific sections:

- The first section provides you with an overview of the topic
- The Implications section discusses why the concept is important, and why it is important to learn and apply.
- The Strategies, Tips & Techniques to Apply section teaches how to use and apply the particular concept to your work.
- The Points to Ponder section gives you something to think about or to be discussed with a group setting. These are questions not meant to be immediately answered, but to be pondered over time.
- The Training Activity section provides you with the tools to transfer what you have learned to your job. It is designed to help create an action plan to effectively apply the concept.

Each of the topics in this series is time-tested and proven in the marketplace. They have been used by thousands of employees as training tools. Many of the users have commented that what made these books valuable, was the ability to refer to them when a problem surfaced. They indicated that they remembered reading about the exact problem. They referred back to these books and found an appropriate solution.

You will find them equally valuable as a resource in your professional development library.

Table of Contents

LEARNING OBJECTIVES:

- To understand the importance of developing customer confidence.
- To understand how high levels of customer confidence are developed and sustained.
- To analyze factors that impact levels of confidence.
- To develop strategies and techniques that build customer confidence.
- To identify strategies that maintain and sustain high levels of customer confidence.
- To leverage customer confidence to develop additional opportunities.

1

The Importance of Customer Confidence in Sales

Whether making a new sale or working with an existing customer, the level of confidence or trust established between the customer and the salesperson is the foundation of the relationship.

IMPLICATIONS – WHAT THIS MEANS TO YOU

If a customer or prospect has little or no confidence in a salesperson and their company, it is highly unlikely he or she will be given any valuable time. Too much is at stake in business today to waste time on these individuals. Conversely, if the prospect or customer has developed a heightened sense of trust and confidence, they can become strong advocates and loyal customers.

Customer confidence plays a critical role in sales. Every action and word said by a salesperson has a direct impact on the level of trust and confidence a prospect or customer has. The correlation between trust, confidence and loyalty is a strong one. Salespeople should be keenly aware that they all have ramifications on their ability to sell successfully.

STRATEGIES, TIPS & TECHNIQUES TO APPLY

Salespeople who have developed a strong sense of prospect or customer confidence have created a bond of trust that has positive ramifications to the sales relationship, including:

Reduced Sales Resistance

The majority of sales stalls, objections and barriers stem directly from a lack of faith in the salesperson. In many instances the salesperson rushed the sale and failed to adequately qualify and develop the prospect, or was unsuccessful in educating the prospect and reducing the risk in their mind enough to make the purchase.

Salespeople who invest the time to build trust and rapport understand the central importance of customer confidence to the sale and overall relationship. They know that without a foundation of trust, sales will not be made. Once prospect or customer confidence is established, salespeople will see resistance melt away. The prospect may have concerns and questions over legitimate issues, but many of the meaningless objections, stalls and barriers will disappear.

Salespeople should not confuse rapport building with trust and confidence. Rapport building is important. It is the starting point of getting to know the prospect and establishing trust. However, trust and customer confidence go far beyond discussing sports and hobbies or the other typical approaches often used by salespeople to build rapport.

Faster Selling Cycles

When confidence is established, salespeople will find that the customer wants to do business with them. Many of the objections and barriers have been eliminated, but salespeople will find that other bureaucratic elements that might have slowed the sales process have also been removed. Once a prospect has made the emotional decision and has confidence in the salesperson and in his or her decision, it is surprising how fast things can move.

Decreased Competition

While the actual number of competitors remains unchanged, a prospect or customer who has developed a strong sense of trust and confidence is less likely to consider other suppliers until the point when his or her faith in the salesperson and their company wanes. Obviously, there is a strong correlation between a prospect's or customer's trust and confidence and customer loyalty. Both go hand in hand.

It should be noted that there are various levels of customer confidence ranging from enough to place an order to strong trust and confidence that fosters fierce customer loyalty. It is the responsibility of the salesperson to continue to build and nurture customer confidence to lock the customer into a solid relationship.

Decreased Post-Sales Problems

While increased customer confidence will not reduce or eliminate post-sales problems stemming from installation, training and initial implementation, a heightened confidence that problems will be handled promptly and efficiently will lessen their impact.

Increased customer confidence shapes the perception that the salesperson will do whatever is necessary to deliver satisfaction to the customer and meet and exceed his or her personal expectations. It changes the complexion of the post-sales landscape. With heightened confidence levels, the customer is not looking for nor anticipating problems. Minor problems are overlooked.

Increased Retention

Some salespeople are able to develop high levels of customer confidence, while others struggle in this pursuit. One way or another, the salesperson who invests the time and energy to continue to build and foster customer confidence in his or her company, products and them personally will see increased levels of customer retention.

Salespeople should not minimize this: according to a Harvard Business School study, a 2% retention of the existing customer base equates to a 10% decrease in operating expenses.

Increased Satisfaction

For all of the reasons listed above and because of the customer's heightened confidence levels, he or she has an expectation of overall satisfaction.

It should be carefully noted by salespeople that any failure to live up to the level of a customer's confidence will result in an even deeper fall from their good graces. In these instances, the salesperson has not only failed to produce the promised results and meet the customer's expectations, but also he or she has betrayed the customer's confidence and trust. Once trust and confidence is betrayed, it is extremely difficult to regain the customer's business.

POINTS TO PONDER — SOMETHING TO THINK ABOUT

1. Have you considered the importance of customer confidence in relation to the success of a sale?
2. Have you ever experienced the loss of a customer's confidence? Explain what happened.

TRAINING ACTIVITY — APPLICATION & ACTION PLAN

Determine the steps, actions and activities that you need to undertake to continually build a customer's confidence in your company, products and yourself.

2

Factors that Affect a Customer's Confidence

There are a number of variables and factors that can affect a prospect's or customer's confidence in a salesperson. Each individual develops an intuition about the people they deal with. The intuition is the prospect's or customer's ability to subconsciously process countless amounts of data and input that they are receiving about the salesperson.

IMPLICATIONS – WHAT THIS MEANS TO YOU

Without the ability to psychoanalyze each individual prospect and customer, it is difficult to know exactly what criteria he or she uses to evaluate a salesperson. Each brings specific sets of filters or experiences that influence and impact their levels of confidence in the salesperson.

While salespeople have no way of knowing how they are being evaluated by a customer, they can control the factors and criteria that are associated with establishing and building a prospect's confidence in them. While they may not cover every factor, they can be assured that they are doing the things that build confidence in the vast majority of prospects and customers.

STRATEGIES, TIPS & TECHNIQUES TO APPLY

The degree of confidence and trust a salesperson generates is defined by their actions. While anyone can make statements and pronouncements, individuals are ultimately judged on their actions. Salespeople must uphold high standards of integrity and personal behavior if they are to foster and nurture trust with their customers. Whether they realize it or not, every word and action is being closely observed and scrutinized. Trust and customer confidence are measured according to the following criteria:

Reputation

The personal and professional reputation of the salesperson and their company and its products and services can have an impact on the prospect's confidence and expectations.

A prior reputation can be established through the advertising, marketing and positioning efforts of the salesperson's company. These can result in a positive reputation and a heightened sense of confidence as the salesperson walks through the door.

A prior reputation can also be established by scandals and news stories that paint a mental picture in the prospect's mind, such as the problems experienced by Enron and Arthur Andersen. In this case the salesperson has to surmount a large barrier just to overcome the lack of prospect confidence.

Previous Experiences

Salespeople should be aware that a customer's or prospect's confidence level could be strongly influenced by their prior experiences with a competitor or similar type of company. Negative experiences can produce negative expectations and a diminished sense of confidence despite the salesperson's efforts to build it.

A prospect's or customer's negative experiences are often hidden or unknown to salespeople unless they take the time to ask about them. Otherwise they can produce a series of hidden agendas that salespeople will find difficult to anticipate and handle.

Professionalism

The professionalism of the salesperson either builds or undermines a prospect's or customer's confidence. While professionalism can mean many different things to different people, in this case it is the attitude, demeanor and manner by which a salesperson handles him or herself in front of the prospect of customer.

Prospects and customers have specific expectations and perceptions of how a salesperson should treat them and handle him or herself. Common examples might include relationship building, qualifying, developing and identifying needs and taking the time to develop a quality solution. When the salesperson does not meet these expectations in the prospect or customer's eyes, then their perceived professionalism suffers.

Promises and Commitments

One common customer frustration has to do with the number of promises made by salespeople versus those kept. Competitors barrage customers and prospects with promises they never deliver on. It is so pervasive that many prospects and customers become numb to the specter of another promise.

Most customers are amazed when a salesperson actually keeps a promise. As simple as this might seem, this can truly distinguish a salesperson.

Problem Resolution

No prospect or customer expects a salesperson or their company to be perfect. They all accept that problems will occur as a natural part of the process. However, they expect a prompt response and to have their problem resolved in a timely manner.

Quick and efficient problem resolution builds customer confidence and intensifies loyalty. This offers salespeople the best opportunity to cement their customer's relationships with them.

Expertise and Experience

Initial prospect and customer confidence is developed by their perception of the salesperson's competence, expertise and experience. While in past decades buyers would tolerate a novice salesperson with minimal knowledge and experience, in today's competitive environment, competence, expertise and experience provide the salesperson with a license to sell, but not a guarantee for the order.

If prospects and customers perceive a noticeable lack of competence, it will take the salesperson an appreciable amount of effort to build their confidence to the point where a sale is possible.

Personal Appearance

The salesperson's personal appearance does have an impact on customer confidence. Every individual makes countless personal judgments about his or her environment. Most of these are perceptions and judgments that are occurring subconsciously, yet they form the initial criteria that a prospect or customer will use to determine the level of trust he or she will have in a salesperson. These perceptions are formed by the physical attributes, appearance, dress, speech patterns, diction and nonverbal communication patterns of the salesperson.

It should be noted that each individual has their internal biases that have been molded since childhood and that form the basis of any internal judgments.

Confidentiality

Increasingly, as more salespeople are involved in consultative sales, they must demonstrate their ability to respect and honor confidential and sensitive information shared by a prospect or customer.

The foundation of a strong customer partnership is built on the confidentiality shared between the customer and salesperson. This is where information and expertise is imparted and where the true basis of trust and confidence is established.

POINTS TO PONDER – SOMETHING TO THINK ABOUT

1. How would you rate your personal level of trustworthiness as perceived by your prospects and customers?
2. How would you evaluate the levels of confidence your customers have in you?

TRAINING ACTIVITY – APPLICATION & ACTION PLAN

1. Perform a self-analysis regarding trust. On a sheet of paper list the following:
    - Professionalism
    - Promises and Commitments
    - Previous Experiences
    - Reputation
    - Problem Resolution
    - Expertise and Experience
    - Personal Appearance
    - Communications
    - Confidentiality
2. Next to each category, list the ways you can increase your personal levels of trust and confidence with your prospects and customers.
3. Identify the actions you need to take to implement your ideas.

3

Customer Problems that Can Be Encountered

Most salespeople are instructed on the value and need to build trust and rapport with a prospect. Many diligently apply the lessons learned only to find that they are not selling in a perfect world. The concepts of trust, rapport and customer confidence imply that a relationship is created when in fact there are many cases where a sustainable relationship is not possible with a prospective client.

IMPLICATIONS — WHAT THIS MEANS TO YOU

Most salespeople find that in the real world, there are prospects and customers who do lie and cannot be trusted. These are individuals where mutual trust and respect cannot be achieved, much less sustained.

Salespeople must sell to people in positions of power and influence who can make their lives miserable. They must realize that not all individuals are trustworthy and that developing a level of customer confidence with every prospect is nearly impossible. Nothing the salesperson can or will do will ever satisfy these individuals.

STRATEGIES, TIPS & TECHNIQUES TO APPLY

Difficult prospects can cause serious problems for salespeople, especially when the individuals involved are in positions of power and influence at a major account and it is nearly impossible for the salesperson to walk away.

Some of the more common situations salespeople can encounter include:

Problems with Trust

Salespeople will encounter prospects or customers who cannot be trusted because they are unethical and lack personal integrity.

Often these individuals don't openly display these behaviors, but will say one thing to a salesperson and do the complete opposite. Unfortunately many salespeople don't learn about these individuals until they have been able to cause them some harm. They only learn about them once their trust has been betrayed.

Personal Agendas

It is not uncommon for salespeople to get caught in the middle of internal political infighting, turf wars and individuals pushing their personal agendas.

The outcomes of these internal conflicts can determine who ultimately wins or loses the sale. The results can have no bearing on the quality, pricing or capabilities of the winning vendor. The only thing that matters is the side that wins the political wars and the luck of the draw of the vendor who picked the right individual.

Salespeople who gain sales in these circumstances should be on the alert. Because the sale was won due to the influence and power of a faction within the prospect's company that won, salespeople should be aware that other factions will actively work against them—not because they are not a qualified supplier, but because they were awarded the sale based on political influence.

Game Playing

There are individuals who for their own reasons like to play games with those they come into contact with. These individuals can cause real havoc with salespeople because their responses can change at a whim and completely contradict their previous words and actions.

Salespeople find these people difficult to gauge because they are contradictory for no apparent reason. There is no rationale or agenda that appears to underpin these individuals' actions.

Internally Focused Prospects and Customers

When salespeople cannot understand what is going on, they can explore the self-centeredness and selfishness of the individual they are dealing with.

There are individuals that are so "I-focused" that nothing else matters. All of their motivation and actions center around them. These individuals can be quite dangerous because they are capable of doing anything that promotes them and their agenda.

Actions Salespeople Can Take

In most of the circumstances listed above, the situation can get quickly out of hand and beyond the salesperson's capacity to properly manage it. However there are specific preventative actions that can be taken:

1. Salespeople should document everything these customers and prospects say and do in a sales diary. Contemporaneous notes can be used to document their actions to advisors and managers who will be needed to be called upon to assist the salesperson.
2. Salespeople should ask for outside assistance to deal with these individuals. Sometimes a change in faces and personalities can alleviate the situation. At the very least, other individuals can verify the problem and brainstorm potential solutions.
3. Salespeople should not confront these individuals, but they can use their contemporaneous notes to restrict the activities that are causing the problems. When faced with the facts, these individuals find it difficult to cover their actions.
4. Salespeople should allow managers and advisors to make the decision as to what to do with these individuals and the account. Sometimes senior managers can be called upon to talk with a counterpart in the prospect's company with the intention of working around this individual or circumstance.

5. If the decision to walk away from the prospect needs to be made, salespeople should allow their managers to make the choice.

POINTS TO PONDER – SOMETHING TO THINK ABOUT

1. What has been your personal experiences with dishonest, unethical prospects or customers who lack integrity?
2. How have you personally handled problematic customers?

TRAINING ACTIVITY – APPLICATION & ACTION PLAN

1. Identify specific situations with problem customers that you have encountered and describe how you handled them. Indicate whether the outcome was positive or negative.
2. Determine from your observations how well you can handle these types of customer problems.
    - Problems with Trust
    - Personal Agendas
    - Game Playing
    - Control Issues
    - Internally Focused Prospects and Customers

4

When Customer Confidence Is Violated

What options are available to the salesperson when a customer situation has deteriorated to the point where there is little or no hope of recovering a lost piece of business? Each situation is different and there are certain steps that should be taken before the salesperson gives up on the account.

IMPLICATIONS – WHAT THIS MEANS TO YOU

Even when an account appears lost, salespeople must take some final action steps. While this may not recover the lost business, it can stabilize the customer and prevent them from taking other actions that can have a rippling negative impact on the salesperson's sales with other customers. Additionally, a final effort by the salesperson can leave his or her customer with a positive impression that can be used to reestablish the relationship over time. No salesperson can afford to leave an account in disarray with unresolved problems and issues. This only leaves the customer with ammunition to prevent the salesperson from ever getting back into the account. It also can be used to justify their position and harm the salesperson's reputation in the eyes of other customers.

STRATEGIES, TIPS & TECHNIQUES TO APPLY

Certain selling situations will deteriorate to the point that the customer has become angry and increasingly hostile and refuses to deal with the salesperson. In a customer environment that is highly unstable and continues to deteriorate, there are some corrective actions a salesperson can take. It should be noted that when the relationship has reached this point, the chances of recovery are minimal. However, it is still important to stabilize the situation and prevent any more damage from occurring.

Bring in a Fresh Face

When trust and rapport have been destroyed, it may be helpful to bring in another individual to deal with the customer. Not only is the customer dealing with a fresh face, but they are also dealing with new perspectives and insights into the problem. A sales manager or different salesperson can be called upon and prove effective in certain situations. Sometimes these individuals are able to remove emotionalism from negotiations. They may prove good substitutes for allowing the customer to vent and in certain instances begin to rebuild lost trust, communication and rapport.

Bring in Reinforcements

Depending upon the size of the account, it may be necessary to bring in senior managers and technical specialists to resolve the problem. While the customer may not reestablish the relationship, they will notice the commitment the supplier has made to resolve their problem. With certain personality types, these actions may assuage their egos and make them feel more in control.

Stabilize the Situation

At the very least, the salesperson must stabilize the customer's situation. This requires rectifying the problem and resolving any lingering issues. While the customer has been lost, the situation has been resolved to the point where the customer's complaints have been stopped. This provides a positive environment to be reestablished once the customer has calmed down.

Counter Any Customer Activism

It is essential that the customer does not turn into an activist against the supplier. There are two extremes in customer relationships. The most desirable is when the customer becomes an advocate so impressed with a supplier that they go out and actively promote their business. The opposite extreme is the activist. An activist is so angry with a supplier that they will do everything in their power to not only badmouth but also actively work against and harm their business.

Salespeople must do whatever it takes to prevent an unhappy customer from becoming an activist. This is why it is critical to stabilize the situation and resolve all issues even if the business is lost. If the customer does turn into an activist, the salesperson can counter their actions with a clear and concise explanation of what happened and the actions they took to resolve their problems. A reasonable person can judge for him or herself whether or not the activist's actions were warranted. It should be noted that an activist can cause a lot of damage, and a salesperson needs to prevent this from happening at all costs.

Slowly Reestablish the Relationship

Once the customer's situation has been stabilized, the salesperson can slowly begin to reestablish trust and rapport. When these are broken, it will take a great deal of time to rebuild a solid foundation. When the events that lead up to the loss of business are out of the salesperson's control, the timeline may be shortened. If the salesperson was directly involved, it may not happen at all.

Walk Away and Wait

There are instances when the salesperson has no realistic choice but to walk away and wait. The customer may feel so betrayed that they will never allow the salesperson to return. If this occurs, the only option is to hope that the customer gets replaced and that the new buyer will be more receptive. With rapid changes happening in most industries. this is more of a possibility than in past decades when buyers remained in a permanent position for years.

POINTS TO PONDER — SOMETHING TO THINK ABOUT

1. What has been your personal attitude once an account is lost? Do you leave it or do you attempt to stabilize it before you move on? Explain.
2. What personal experiences have you had when dealing with a lost account? How do these experiences affect your perspectives on this issue? Explain.

TRAINING ACTIVITY — APPLICATION & ACTION PLAN

Identify a damaged customer relationship that appears to be heading toward a loss of business or is beyond repair. This can be an existing or historic account.

1. Perform a lost account evaluation of what actions were taken to recover the account.
    a. Determine if any actions were taken after the account appeared to be lost.
    b. Were all problems and issues addressed and resolved?
    c. Were there any specific actions taken to stabilize the account?
    d. Was everything done to assure that the account was left in a positive state?
2. Determine if any additional actions need to be taken to begin the reestablishment of trust and rapport.

5

Establishing Trust, Confidence and Credibility

One of the primary reasons prospects are reluctant to buy from a salesperson is a lack of trust, confidence and credibility in the salesperson and their company and product.

First impressions do count, so it is important that salespeople quickly establish credibility and buyer confidence, or they will be plagued by these concerns all through the sales process. This will result in wasted time and resources and numerous objections to the sale.

IMPLICATIONS – WHAT THIS MEANS TO YOU

Many salespeople perceive building trust and rapport as a simple exercise allowing them to find something in common with the customer to talk about. While that may provide an icebreaker to initiate a conversation, salespeople who wish to develop strong levels of trust and credibility must demonstrate the clear value of their expertise and experience to the prospect or customer.

Credibility and trust in the salesperson's abilities are based upon demonstrating what he or she can do for the prospect or customer to benefit them based upon highlighting what was successfully done for other customers.

The prospect or customer is only interested in what the salesperson's product or service will do for them. Small talk may be entertaining, but clients want results.

STRATEGIES, TIPS & TECHNIQUES TO APPLY

Customer perceptions and expectations underlie all sales situations. The strategies detailed below address these key points and resolve many of the problems often encountered during the course of the selling process.

Presentation and preparation create confidence in the prospect's mind that they are dealing with a professional salesperson and a competent company. The smart salesperson who pays attention to these details throughout discussions will discover the process will be smoother and more time efficient.

There are several specific strategies a salesperson can employ to firmly establish credibility and develop buyer confidence. These include:

Adequate Preparation

A salesperson should be prepared for every call and appointment with a prospective customer. This includes having answers and responses to deal with every contingency.

Customer Involvement

A prospective buyer should be personally involved early in the presentation. Touching, feeling, examining or using a product is an excellent way to get the prospect involved.

Salespeople should ask how a product or service might be used or applied to improve their business. This focuses the customer's mind on the positive aspects of the product.

Sales Expertise

The salesperson creates credibility and establishes confidence with his or her knowledge and expertise. This is demonstrated by the breadth and scope of the answers he or she provides to the prospect's questions. It is also demonstrated by the ability to ask the right questions by probing to identify the customer's needs and concerns.

Statements of Proof

Salespeople should use articles about their company from newspapers and trade journals to establish immediate credibility. These demonstrate a third party acceptance of credibility by independent sources.

Customer Case Studies and Testimonials

Salespeople should use case studies of a previous customer's success with their product or service. Customers and prospects feel more comfortable when they know they are not the only company buying a specific product. If they specifically know a company or individual who uses the product or service, they may feel comfortable enough to call and discuss the product or service. This provides independent substantiation of the salesperson's claims.

If a large nationally recognized company is using the salesperson's product or service, this establishes immediate credibility since their buying criteria is often more complex and demanding.

Customer Documentation

It is important for salespeople to document their statements and claims. This can be done by providing a list of satisfied customers for the prospect to call. Additionally, a binder of customer letters and testimonials should be used to demonstrate the value of the salesperson's product and service.

Having a written presentation organized by key points, features, benefits and objections can prove helpful. As they come up during a presentation, salespeople can simply refer to the prepared section to answer a prospect's concerns and objections.

Prepared responses to a concern and objection are extremely valuable and should not be underestimated. A strong response made by a salesperson establishes confidence and credibility while short-circuiting any further objections. A weak and unprepared response invites further scrutiny.

Emphasize Key Points

Several key points need to be emphasized with all prospects including:

Customer Focus – Salespeople should emphasize their focus on meeting the customer's needs and concerns. Customers have expectations that need to be identified and met.

Sales presentations should be built on this focus and imply the development of a long-term relationship with the prospect. If the prospect perceives that the salesperson is only there for the commission instead of establishing a long-term relationship, he or she will resist the sale.

Service After the Sale – Customers often fear the salesperson will disappear after the sale. Salespeople should emphasize delivery, installation, training, service and troubleshooting after the sale.

Problems will occur. Salespeople should address the question, "If a problem does occur, this is what will specifically happen. I will personally..."

POINTS TO PONDER – SOMETHING TO THINK ABOUT

1. What strategies have you employed to establish trust, confidence and credibility with your customers? Explain.
2. Is there a unique manner or method that you can use to establish trust and credibility with your prospects and customers?

TRAINING ACTIVITY – APPLICATION & ACTION PLAN

Develop a sales portfolio that you can use to demonstrate your value to your prospects and customers. Include in it:

- Magazine and trade journal articles on your product or company
- Testimonials

- Case studies
- Customer references
- Any additional support materials

6

Moving the Customer from Trust to Confidence

While the establishment of trust and rapport is an essential element in moving the sale forward and obtaining an order, confidence is required to develop the relationship, build loyalty and retain the customer's business over the long term.

This is a critical area many salespeople can overlook in a race to generate sales and commissions, yet can yield a great deal of success with less effort.

IMPLICATIONS — WHAT THIS MEANS TO YOU

There is a certain kind of salesperson whose primary focus is to get the sale and move on to the next prospect without any concern for overall customer satisfaction and retention. Unfortunately there are a large number of these salespeople, and the often unethical and manipulative tactics they employ leave customers and prospects with a bitter taste and an overall mistrust of the rest of the salespeople they must deal with.

These types of salespeople appear successful and are often envied by colleagues, yet they lack a solid foundation of happy and satisfied customers to build upon.

The astute salesperson understands that lasting success is sustained with a solid customer base. He or she understands the best source of new business is not necessarily developed from the next prospect but from the development of new and existing opportunities within the current customer base. This business can only be developed when the salesperson has earned the customer's trust and confidence.

STRATEGIES, TIPS & TECHNIQUES TO APPLY

Once trust and rapport are established, salespeople are able to move prospects to the point of commitment where an order is placed and they transition into customers. However, customer relationships must be nurtured to the point where satisfaction is delivered and value received. This is accomplished when salespeople focus on building on the following elements:

Reliability

Salespeople have sullied their profession's reputation for reliability. Many quickly disappear after the sale without regard for the customer, failing to realize that while the sale might be over for them, it is only beginning for the customer.

The customer expects the salesperson to be there to facilitate the order, make sure the kinks and problems are worked out and that things run smoothly. While customers understand the human factor associated with any sale will lead to problems, they also expect the salesperson to be there to fix whatever needs to be fixed quickly and efficiently. When salespeople do this successfully, they are seen as reliable. Customers learn that they can count on the salesperson to stand up for them, watch out for problems, and anticipate their needs. This builds their confidence in the salesperson.

Credibility

The salesperson's credibility is determined on two planes. First is the professional credibility of the salesperson. This is the perception that the salesperson is competent and qualified to sell his or her product and represent their company. This is determined by the expertise and experience exhibited by the salesperson.

The second area is the personal credibility of the salesperson. This is the perception that the salesperson is true to their words and that promises made are promises kept.

When salespeople have credibility, the customer learns that they can count on what is being said as being believable and that the salesperson will stand behind what they say and promise.

Respect

Salespeople earn a customer's respect through their words, actions, reliability and integrity. While these factors have a lessening effect in many sectors of public and political life, they are still paramount in the sales profession.

Focus

A customer's confidence can be affected by the salesperson's focus. Salespeople who are internally focused are concerned with making the next sale and collecting their commission. They often do what needs to be done to get the sale with little regard for the customer and the consequences of their actions.

The salesperson who is focused on external needs of the customer garners his or her confidence. These salespeople have placed their customers' needs ahead of their own. Customers quickly learn that these salespeople value their business and consider them to be important. This builds their confidence in the salesperson.

Confidence

The combination of the elements listed above builds a customer's confidence. However, there are salespeople who automatically exude a sense of confidence to the customer through their actions, self-confidence and professionalism. Customers are drawn to these salespeople and want to do business with them. There is an imperceptible sense of confidence in these individuals.

POINTS TO PONDER – SOMETHING TO THINK ABOUT

1. What ways do you build on a customer's trust to establish confidence?
2. Can you identify ways that undermine the customer's trust without betraying him or her?

TRAINING ACTIVITY – APPLICATION & ACTION PLAN

1. On a sheet of paper, list the following elements in a column:
    - Reliability
    - Credibility
    - Respect
    - Focus
    - Confidence
2. Evaluate your own actions to determine if your actions build customer confidence.
    a. Look at each area and identify any areas of potential weakness.
    b. Determine what actions need to be taken to strengthen each area of weakness.
    c. Create an action plan and implement it for each item identified.

7

Helping Prospects to Make the Leap of Faith

All salespeople are aware of the importance of establishing trust and rapport with a prospective customer. Many use the well-worn technique of looking around the prospect's office and initiating a discussion about some object or picture of obvious importance to the prospect.

The concept of rapport and relationship building goes beyond a surface discussion of obvious items of interest. If the salesperson doesn't have a real interest in the item, the motivation becomes transparent, and aside from breaking the ice, it does little to build rapport and establish trust with the prospect.

IMPLICATIONS – WHAT THIS MEANS TO YOU

Astute salespeople understand it is an act of faith on the part of the prospect to buy their product. The buying decision goes beyond the building of surface rapport to the development of trust and credibility. The prospect is making a number of critical decisions about the salesperson, the company he or she represents, the product he or she sells and the perceptions and expectations created during the sales process. The development of a personal relationship might enhance the decision to buy, but the decision goes beyond whether a prospect likes the salesperson.

It is important for salespeople to appreciate that a commitment to buy can have numerous ramifications for the decision maker. He or she is committing company financial resources, and if the product or service doesn't work or has problems, the fault will lie with them. In the current business and economic environment, depending upon the size of the financial commitment, the consequences to the decision maker can be dire. Consequently, he or she must be absolutely sure of their decision and have confidence in the salesperson before a sale can be made.

STRATEGIES, TIPS & TECHNIQUES TO APPLY

The following factors build foundations of trust that lead to sales. Salespeople are asking the prospect to take a leap of faith. He or she must trust the salesperson before they will do it.

The ultimate buying decision hinges on whether the prospect believes in the product and the representations of the salesperson. The credibility of both is determined by four factors:

Consistency

Every decision an individual makes is based upon their prior experiences first with the salesperson, then his or her company and the performance of its product. If there is a basis of positive experience, then the representations made about future performance are believable. If there have been problems, credibility could be an issue. It depends on how the problems are resolved: while problems are acceptable, customers and prospects expect a rapid response to resolve the problem when it occurs.

The next element prospects consider is their overall experience with other vendors. These experiences—especially if other vendors have underperformed—can certainly taint the prospect's opinions and cause additional credibility problems for the salesperson. This can happen even if the salesperson or their company were not directly responsible for the previous problems.

Unless the prospect volunteers this information, salespeople might not be aware of how previous experiences are impacting the current sale. Therefore, it is important for salespeople to probe to determine if these experiences even exist. Once uncovered, salespeople must discuss these experiences and address the concerns with the prospect.

Credibility

Salespeople hold a tremendous amount of power to create and shape perceptions and expectations in the prospect's mind. Many salespeople don't understand how to control this power. Usually they use puff and exaggerations to sell their products, creating perceptions and expectations they are unable to meet.

Since everything salespeople say, present and represent creates a perception and expectation in the prospect's mind, the perceptions and expectations can become incredible and unbelievable. When this happens, credibility becomes an issue in the prospect's mind.

Salespeople must be aware of the perceptions and expectations they create and how each impacts a prospect's thinking. Properly done, the perceptions and expectations a salesperson creates can greatly enhance his or her credibility and lead the prospect toward the sale.

Congruency

Salespeople must create a unified message in everything they do. The salesperson who builds a perception and expectation of a quality product sends a mixed message with a bargain basement price. Everything said, presented and done must fit together and make logical sense to the prospect. A failure to do so creates a sense of mistrust in the prospect's mind.

Common Ground

Trust is established when there is common ground between individuals. This goes beyond the capacity of initial surface rapport building and is based upon legitimately similar interests or backgrounds. This may include attending the same school, coming from the same city, belonging to the same fraternal or civic organizations, etc. These are the common grounds where a real bond can be established with the prospect.

POINTS TO PONDER — SOMETHING TO THINK ABOUT

1. What has occurred when you attempted to close a sale before you developed a bond of trust with a prospect? Explain.
2. What additional techniques have you used to develop trust and rapport with a prospect?

TRAINING ACTIVITY — APPLICATION & ACTION PLAN

1. Examine the following factors to see how well you are able to build trust, rapport and confidence with your prospects. "Common ground" is to be considered on a case-by-case basis.
    - Consistency
    - Credibility
    - Congruency
2. Identify areas that might be causing problems or sending a mixed message.
3. Determine what needs to be done to align your words and actions.

8

How Customer Confidence Impacts Their Decisions

When high degrees of customer confidence are obtained, customers view the salesperson in a different light, and this changes their decision making in a way that favors the salesperson as long as the trust is maintained.

IMPLICATIONS — WHAT THIS MEANS TO YOU

Customer decisions are made when they consider a number of variables. However, when salespeople build and nurture bonds of trust to the point that customers have high levels of confidence, this impacts how a buying decision is made and has the capacity of altering the entire relationship between the customer and the salesperson.

When customers have confidence in and trust their salespeople, it creates a relationship with distinct advantages as well as responsibilities. The customer trusts the salesperson's input and weighs his or her advice more heavily than during the initial sales process. He or she is perceived to be a member of the customer's team, and decisions are made accordingly.

STRATEGIES, TIPS & TECHNIQUES TO APPLY

Salespeople who have fostered a high level of customer confidence have attained an enviable position that provides them with a great deal of leverage with the customer that places them in a strong competitive position. This position allows them to defend their position against competitive efforts to sell the account. These advantages include:

Increased Satisfaction

Customer confidence translates to higher levels of customer satisfaction. Customers are confident that the salesperson is capable of repeatedly meeting and exceeding their expectations. They are satisfied with the value the salesperson has delivered and are confident that this value will be sustained in all future transactions. They feel confident that if there is a problem it will be handled quickly, competently, and to their satisfaction. This equates to a strong competitive advantage for the salesperson that positively impacts the customer's future decisions regarding the continuation of the relationship. While the customer might entertain competitive offers, the salesperson maintains an advantage. This advantage can be further amplified by the following factors:

Reduced Resistance – When customer confidence is achieved, salespeople will encounter reduced levels of resistance from the customer. A strong relationship and bond of trust between the customer and salesperson underscores that the salesperson will not take advantage of the customer. Because of this relationship of trust, the customer's skepticism is removed as well as many of the barriers and objections the salesperson would otherwise encounter when attempting to make additional sales.

Receptiveness – Salespeople will find that with a relationship of trust, they are viewed as a consultative partner who is looking out for the customer's well-being. In this capacity, the customer will be more receptive to new ideas, insights, feedback and observations made by the salesperson even if they result in additional sales for him or her.

This places the salesperson in a position where the competition does not have the opportunity to counter additional efforts to expand the business and introduce new applications.

Expanded Opportunities

Increased customer confidence places the salesperson in another enviable position. Research has shown that current suppliers are not automatically considered for new opportunities unless they are actively involved with the customer and seek them out.

However, when salespeople have developed a strong bond of trust and have earned the position as a consultative member of the customer's team, they are often privy to the planning of new opportunities. This gives them the inside track over the competition and the ability to influence specifications so that they favor their product or service.

Increased Expectations

One factor that salespeople need to consider when they have established a strong bond of trust with a customer is that they are then expected to provide a higher level of service and satisfaction. When bonds of trust are established, expectations rise.

This has the potential of being abused by the customer who may expect the salesperson to deliver additional services or favors without further price increases to cover them. While higher expectations of service can cement the customer relationship, salespeople should avoid being placed in positions where the customer uses them to their own advantage.

POINTS TO PONDER — SOMETHING TO THINK ABOUT

1. What changes in a customer's decision making process have you observed when their levels of confidence have increased?
2. What other advantages have you experienced when you developed a strong level of customer confidence?

TRAINING ACTIVITY — APPLICATION & ACTION PLAN

1. Select one account where customer confidence is sustained.
2. Select one account where customer confidence has not been attained.
3. Compare the two accounts and contrast the differences using the following criteria:
    - Satisfaction
    - Resistance
    - Receptiveness
    - Opportunities
    - Expectations

About the Author

Timothy F. Bednarz, Ph.D. is CEO of the American Management Development Group, Inc. For over 20 years he has researched, designed and authored hundreds of learning and development programs used by Fortune 1000 companies.

He is also the author of *Great! What Makes Leaders Great. What They Did, How They Did It and What You Can Learn from It* (2011).

Speaking Availability

Timothy F. Bednarz, Ph.D. is available for speaking engagements for your next meeting or association event. He can be contacted at 800-654-4935 or by e-mail at timothy.bednarz@majorium.com.

Bulk Sales

Bulk sales of this book or any other titles available from Majorium Business Press. Inquiries can be directed to sales@majorium.com, or by phone at 800-6654-4935.

Quick Order Form

Fax orders: 715-342-1118. Send this form.

Telephone orders: Call 800-654-4935 toll-free. Have your credit card ready.

Email orders: sales@majorium.com

Postal orders: Majorium Business Press, 2025 Main Street, Stevens Point, WI 54481, USA.

Please send the following books:

____

____

____

____

Please send more FREE information on:

❑Catalog ❑Speaking/Seminars ❑Mailing Lists ❑Consulting

Name: ____________________________________

Address: __________________________________

City: ____________________ State: _____ Zip: ________

Telephone: ________________________________

Email address: _____________________________

Sales tax: Please add 5.5% for products shipped to Wisconsin addresses.

Shipping by air:

United States: $4.00 for first book and $2.00 for each additional product.

International: $9.00 for first book; $5.00 for each additional product (estimate).

Made in United States
Orlando, FL
15 June 2026

82909087R00031